LAST STAND AT STALINGRAD

LAST STAND AT

STALINGRAD

The Battle That Saved the World

EDWARD R. SAMMIS

THE MACMILLAN COMPANY, NEW YORK
COLLIER-MACMILLAN LIMITED, LONDON

*The Macmillan Battle Books are prepared under
the general editorship of Edward R. Sammis.*

Passages from *The Battle for Stalingrad* by Marshal Vasili Chuikov,
translated from the Russian by Harold Silver (English translation,
published in England under the title *The Beginning of the Road: The
Story of the Battle for Stalingrad*, copyright © 1963 by MacGibbon
and Kee, Ltd.), are reprinted by permission of Holt, Rinehart and
Winston, Inc., and MacGibbon and Kee, Ltd.; and from *The Year of
Stalingrad* by Alexander Werth by permission of Alfred A. Knopf, Inc.,
and Hamish Hamilton, Ltd. Selections from war reports that
originally appeared in United Press newspapers are reprinted by
courtesy of United Press International.

PICTURE CREDITS: Imperial War Museum, London, 62–63; Novosti Press
Agency, Moscow, title page, 32, 42, 54, 61, 77, 85; Pictorial Parade, 22,
74–75; Sovfoto, 16, 21, 24, 26, 27, 35, 37, 40, 41, 46, 49 (from USSR Magazine),
51, 53, 66, 67, 71, 78, 83, 88, 90; United Press International, 8, 44;
Wide World, 11, 15, 18, 31, 48, 59, 69, 82. Picture research by
Patricia Crum.

Maps by Romer-Todd
Printed in the United States of America
First Printing

Contents

ONE   THE GERMAN TIDE   7

TWO   "RAT WAR" IN THE CELLARS   34

THREE   "SHELLS AND BOMBS
          FROM MORNING TILL NIGHT"   47

FOUR   COUNTERATTACK   58

FIVE   HITLER'S *GÖTTERDÄMMERUNG*   81

Chronology   91

For Further Reading   94

Index   95

German Offensive *JUNE–AUGUST, 1942*

front line : ———— June 28   - - - - - - August 23

German advances : ⟶ actual   ⟶ projected

temporary diversion of 4th Panzer Army, July 13 : ⟶

The German Tide

Shortly after dawn on the morning of June 19, 1942, a crew of Russians manning an antiaircraft battery near Voronezh on the Eastern Front first heard, then saw an approaching German plane of unusual design.

They recognized it as a Fieseler Storch, a long, tapered high-speed aircraft that the Germans used to transport officers in a hurry from one part to another of the long front, which reached from the Baltic in the north down to the Black Sea.

While the astonished crew looked on, the plane, flying low, came over the no-man's-land between the two lines, executed a sharp turn, and flew along parallel to the Russian position.

The Unexpected Prize

Now it was well within range. Sergeant Pyotr Konyukov gave the order: "Fire!"

A burst of flame, a puff of smoke, and the Storch fell from the sky like a wounded bird just in front of the battery. The gunners ran out at once to see if anyone had survived. They found the pilot dead and one passenger nearly dead. But in a pocket of the plane they discovered something which might prove to be of immense importance. It was a briefcase containing what appeared to be official documents of the utmost secrecy.

Just then there was a rattle of machine-gun fire. A raiding party came out from the German lines to go to the rescue of the fallen plane.

But the Germans were seconds too late. The Russian gunners had already returned to their battery clutching the briefcase.

Sergeant Konyukov lost no time in taking his find to the nearest command post.

Upon studying the documents, the Russian High Command concluded that here was a piece of good fortune almost too good to be true. Here was nothing less than the master plan of the German leader, Adolf Hitler, for his long-awaited all-out offensive against Russia. Now they would know in advance what moves to make, where to concentrate their defense.

But wait.

The flight of the plane into dangerous range, where it was so easily shot down, made the Russians suspicious. Hitler had won

Adolf Hitler, leader of Germany's Nazi Party, with one of his dogs

most of his staggering successes to date against the nations of Western Europe by surprise, feint, and deceit. How were the Russians to know that this was not another one of his tricks, a deliberate chess move to screen a blow in greater force elsewhere?

What were they to make of it? What should be their strategy? They were baffled.

Rise of the Third Reich

So was presented the first enigma in a long series of the grimmest and bloodiest guessing games in history.

From that June day when the German Storch first appeared out of the clouds until the thirty-first of the following January, one puzzle succeeded another. Was the hitherto invincible German Army really strong enough to subdue the world? Or would the Russian people, fired with patriotic fervor, rally their ill-prepared forces in time to drive out the invader as they had driven out Napoleon and others? Why did Hitler, well launched on a strategy that seemed bound to succeed, suddenly abandon it for another one?

In that summer of 1942, Hitler was at the peak of his power. Everything had gone according to his plan.

The whole world was still stunned by the speed and ease of his conquests. Not a German himself but an Austrian, a ne'er-do-well, obscure house painter from a remote village, Hitler had managed to weld the German people into one monstrous machine, then conditioned them blindly to follow him.

Unimpressive in appearance—his toothbrush mustache and the lock of hair falling over his forehead made him a comic figure beyond his own borders, thus obscuring him as a danger —he was nevertheless a golden-tongued, rabble-rousing orator who played on responsive chords of hatred in mobs and whipped them into a chanting frenzy.

Hitler became master of Germany in 1933, using an instrument of his own creation, the Nazi (National Socialist) Party. From that time on he was known as Der Fuehrer (the Leader). In that year also, Hitler established the Third Reich (Realm or Empire), arousing in German hearts their recurring dream of world dominance.

Although the Germans as a people were one of the oldest in Europe, as a nation they were one of the youngest; it was not until the nineteenth century that the various states such as Prussia, Weimar, and others joined together to form what we now know as Germany. According to Hitler's definition, the First Reich was the Holy Roman Empire, a loose confederation of Central European states that flourished in the Middle Ages. The Second Reich came into being during the period of German ascendancy under Bismarck beginning in 1871.

Hitler promised to build the Third Reich so that it would last for a thousand years, with the Germans as masters of the world. Germany had been badly beaten in World War I. As a result, the country had been disarmed and was suffering a deep economic depression. Der Fuehrer's grand promises and plans were eagerly swallowed by a humiliated people—especially by the military, unemployed workers, and small shopkeepers.

Hitler revived the myth of the Germans as the master race. But to whip his mass rallies into a frenzy of hatred, he had to have a scapegoat. The Jews were an easy target because they had worked their way into prominence in the professions, in education, and in business. But he eventually broadened his hatred to include practically all non-Germans—except, of course, the Italians and the Japanese, his Axis partners.

No dream or scheme was too fantastic for his warped imagination and persuasive eloquence to present convincingly. Here was undoubtedly a genius—but a genius dedicated to evil.

RIGHT: *1936—Nazi soldiers parade in Adolf Hitler Plaza in Nuremburg*

The Blitzkrieg

Hitler and the German generals had perfected a technique of modern warfare called the *Blitzkrieg* (Lightning War) that appeared unbeatable.

The *Blitzkrieg* theory was based on the massive use of the latest weapons of scientific warfare—planes, tanks, and mobile guns—manned by highly trained specialists. Launched in surprise attack, the striking force would seize the sensitive points in a country—the power plants, the radio stations, the airports, all the centers of transportation and communication. At a single stroke Hitler could render whole nations helpless.

One country after another had fallen to him—Austria, Poland, Holland, Belgium, France, Czechoslovakia, Norway, Denmark. Only Great Britain was holding out. But London, growing ever wearier, was being pounded by almost nightly air attacks.

As for continental Western Europe, however, Hitler was absolute master from Norway to the Mediterranean. Sweden, Switzerland, Spain, and Turkey, to be sure, still maintained an uneasy neutrality. But they presented no serious problem. His pattern for a world enslaved by Germans was taking shape as he pressed citizens of conquered countries into forced-labor battalions and filled the concentration camps with those who did not fit into his scheme.

Wolf Pack submarines prowled the Atlantic, even torpedoing coast-wise tankers within a few miles of the New Jersey shore. These undersea marauders were endangering the supply lines to Britain, sinking as much as 700,000 tons of Allied shipping in a single month.

In North Africa, Hitler had in General Erwin Rommel—known as the Desert Fox—his most brilliant master of the *Blitzkrieg* technique. Rommel was on the loose, sweeping everything before him with his powerful Afrika Korps of tanks. It looked as though nothing could stop him. By July, 1942, Rommel was within sixty miles of the weakly defended British command headquarters along the Nile in Egypt. If he could accomplish the breakthrough, there would be nothing to prevent him from seizing the rich oil fields of the Middle East. Also, Rommel could then meet the Japanese coming up by way of the Indian Ocean, thus enabling Hitler to join forces for the first time with his Axis partner, who had been invading one country after another in the Eastern world.

Hitler must have gloated that summer. Final victory was just beyond his fingertips.

One great fear had obsessed him from the beginning—that he would someday have to fight on two fronts: in other words, that the United States and Britain might move against him in Europe before he succeeded in knocking Russia out of the war.

He had tried several ways to forestall this possibility. Before setting out to conquer Europe, he had signed a nonaggression pact with his fellow dictator Josef Stalin, Premier of Russia, agreeing that they would not attack each other.

Then in June, 1941, Hitler, accusing Stalin of having violated the pact, staged a surprise attack all along Russia's western border. The suddenness and power of the *Blitzkrieg*, in which thousands of Russian aircraft were destroyed before they could get into the air, badly crippled the Soviet Union. Hitler's armies penetrated almost to Moscow before being thrown back in the winter campaign of 1941–1942.

Now he had reorganized his armies and was ready to strike again with far greater force. He was sure he had learned from his setback. This time, instead of trying to capture Moscow, he would cut through the middle of the country and strike at Stalingrad, southeast of the capital, thereby severing Russian lines of supply and crippling her economy.

Throughout almost every hour and every minute of the six months that followed, he had a chance of succeeding. The struggle could have gone either way.

The Wehrmacht *Invades*

The Battle of Stalingrad may be said to have begun with the shooting down of the Fieseler Storch. The puzzled Russians had not long to wait for the next stage.

Nine days later Hitler's Eastern Front erupted into thunder and lightning with the boom of heavy artillery and the flash of tank guns. The mobile might of the German Army rolled eastward into Russia. It was spearheaded by the fast-moving tanks of the panzer (armored, motorized) divisions, with the support of heavy bombers and light, fast fighter planes—Stukas and Fokkers—all proven stars in Hitler's doomsday firmament.

As the facts were reconstructed later, the loss of the documents had not been planned. The Germans were caught completely off guard by their capture. But since the target day for the complex plan of attack was so near, they had no time to make changes and therefore had no choice but to go ahead.

Hitler was also haunted by another fear beyond having to fight on two fronts—one perhaps even more crucial than the first —namely, that he might run short of gasoline. The tanks, trucks, cars, motorcycles, and planes with which he conducted his Lightning War drank huge quantities of gasoline. It was the lifeblood of a mechanized army. But the great oil fields of the world—in the Middle East, in the Far East, in the United States, in Latin America, and in Russia—were in Allied hands. The stockpiles that Hitler had accumulated before the war and the relatively small amounts of oil that the Germans were able to make from coal would not last forever.

But in southern Russia, in the region known as the Caucasus, on the shores of the Black Sea, were the great oil fields of Baku. Hitler reasoned that if he could capture Baku and at the same time cut Russia in two by seizing Stalingrad, he could strangle the country economically and force her to give up. He could then devote his full attention to making an impregnable fortress out of Western Europe. He could dispose of England at his convenience while he and his Axis partners—Italy and Japan—moved out to capture other vital points and arteries, thus effectively paralyzing every country opposing him.

If he could accomplish this, there seemed to be no reason to doubt that the "master race" could then rule the "mongrel nations" of the rest of the world unchallenged. Indeed, the most minute plans for a world run by Germans, down to details regarding the control of towns and villages in far-distant lands, were revealed in documents found at the Ausländer (Foreign) Institute in Munich.

Wherever the militaristic Nazi "supermen" first appeared, with their high-collared green uniforms, their squarish steel helmets, their fast-firing snub-nosed submachine guns, the very sight of them struck terror in the hearts of the peaceful peoples of Western Europe. The Russians had never fully recovered from Der Fuehrer's surprise attack of the year before. Why

Premier of Russia, Josef Stalin

Der Fuehrer's "supermen" marching during the early days of the war

shouldn't he be able to duplicate his easy conquests of smaller countries on a far larger scale?

Such was Hitler's dream on June 28, 1942, when the crack divisions of the German *Wehrmacht* (War Machine), some 300,000 strong, moved to the attack.

Hitler's Master Plan

In his underground headquarters, known as the Wolf's Lair, in East Prussia (now Poland), Hitler had worked out his strategy down to the smallest detail.

Hitler's plan called for a two-pronged attack. He divided his forces into Army Group A and Army Group B. Army Group

A, under Field Marshal Siegmund List, would head southeast through the Caucasus to seize the oil fields at Baku. Army Group B, under Field Marshal Fedor von Bock, who was later replaced by General Friedrich von Weicks, would plow through the middle of Russia, take Stalingrad, and sever the country in two.

In Army Group B were two star striking forces, composed of veteran divisions—the 4th Panzer (Tank) Army, under Colonel General Hermann Hoth, and the 6th Army, under Colonel General Friedrich von Paulus. Hitler expected much from General Paulus. He had already played a major role in the overrunning of Belgium and Holland. He had also taken part in bringing down France and in the invasion of Poland. And soon the struggle for Stalingrad would claim his undivided attention.

A line officer in World War I, Paulus spent his career in the German Army studying the scientific techniques of modern warfare. Tall (six feet four) and unsmiling, he seemed more a machine than a man. He had but one discernible frailty that marked him as human—a nervous twitch in his left cheek that he found hard to control when under emotional stress.

The City on the Volga

Russia's Mississippi is the Volga, a wide, busy, north-south thoroughfare, the country's principal artery of supply. Situated midway between Moscow and the Caucasus is the city of Stalingrad, sprawling for some thirty-five miles along the Volga's west bank. At this point, Hitler considered Stalingrad as a relatively easy target to be taken in his stride.

The city has a long and picturesque history. As far back as the fifteenth century, it was a strategic point; although formerly a small market town for peasants from the nearby countryside, Tsaritsyn, as it was called, was also a fortress.

The city had seen its share of fighting. In 1919, following the

Bolshevik Revolution, it was attacked by the counterrevolution-aries (who wanted to bring back the Czars) and successfully defended by Josef Stalin as commander of the Red Army. In 1925 Tsaritsyn was renamed Stalingrad in his honor.

As the Communists set about building up their industry, they chose to make a showplace of Stalingrad. Many new factories were located there—metallurgical and electrical shops and tractor plants. By the time of the German attack, it was a busy industrial center with half a million population.

The factories were among the most up to date in all Russia. Located near them were three "garden cities," model communities of houses for workers. Not far away were the finer homes for the "elite"—the new upper class, consisting mostly of Communist Party workers, scientists, and engineers. Facing a central square downtown was a big, modern department store called the Univermag, where the final scene of the drama was to be played out. Also on the square were the club where Party members gathered for meetings and for relaxation, the Red Army House, and official Party headquarters. The city hummed to the rhythm of work. Trams and buses clanged and chugged through the streets taking workers to and from their jobs.

Colonel General Friedrich von Paulus

The people of Stalingrad were proud of their city, proud of its tradition, proud of its accomplishments. They had worked hard to make it the showplace that it was; most of them had seen it grow in their own lifetime.

In the year since the Germans had first invaded, however, Stalingrad had beaten its plowshares into swords. The tractor factories were making tanks now. The citizens were working around the clock, seven days a week, doing their part to swell Russia's badly needed arsenal of weapons.

It was Stalingrad's location that made it important to Hitler, although it was also an important center of communication and supply. If the city remained in Russian hands, it would provide a base from which the Russians could strike at the exposed flanks of either Army Group A or Army Group B. Therefore, it had to be taken.

Hitler's Great Gamble

In those first weeks of the critical summer of 1942, the Russians appeared incapable of offering very much resistance. Hitler's armored panzer divisions roared eastward toward Stalingrad as swiftly and easily as though they were on maneuvers.

The paths of the German armies lay across the vast, empty regions of western Russia. Although known as the steppes, the name is misleading, for here is an almost flat, treeless countryside, not unlike the dusty plains of western Texas, broken only now and then by a ravine or gully.

"As far as the eye can see, the earth is bare," wrote Eugene Krieger, a Russian war correspondent. "For hours you see no house on your way, no tree, no spring with high green grass around—nothing but the boundless plain. . . .

". . . with its dead grass stiff as bristles, with its dust that chokes the people on the roads, with its brackish water and rare wells, with its wind that raises the dust in clouds to mingle with the smoke of the guns . . . the sun is darkened and the day turned into night and men lose touch with each other in the gray noontide fog."

Such a landscape was made to order for the German motorized advance. Tanks and mobile infantry did not have to stick to any road; they could fan out at will in any direction.

On July 13, however, Hitler took a gamble that was later seen to have affected the final outcome of his second Russian campaign. The 4th Panzer Army, which was rapidly approaching Stalingrad from the south, was shifted away from this line of attack to help the 1st Panzers of Army Group A. The tactic didn't work. The 1st, driving toward the oil fields of Baku, arrived at a Don River crossing at the same time as the 4th. The 4th Army only clogged the roads and used up its dwindling supply of gasoline at a faster rate. Ironically, this doubled German force found that the Russians had pulled most of their troops out of the area earlier, and the Nazis had no one to fight. Then Hitler realized his mistake. He ordered Hoth to resume his advance on Stalingrad. But two weeks had gone by. Now it was too late.

Had the 4th Army been allowed to continue according to the original plan, it would almost certainly have captured the city, which at that moment was totally unprepared. As it was, the two-week delay gave the defenders precious time in which to rush up troops and ammunition.

On July 16, after Hitler ordered the 4th Panzers out of their line of attack, he moved his headquarters into the Ukraine at Vinnitsa. Here he could watch the campaign closely and keep a firm hand on the actions of his generals.

"Not One Step Back!"

The speed of the German thrust throughout those hot days of July alarmed not only the Russian War Council but the en-

Soviet infantrymen advancing across a meadow in the Stalingrad area

tire Allied world. Things looked darkest on July 28, when units of Army Group A seized, without much difficulty, the city of Rostov in the southwest, one of the first strongpoints on their way.

Two days later Premier Stalin tried to stiffen the spine of resistance with his famous order to the Red Army: "Not one step back!"

But the Russians fell back even faster than the Germans advanced. Confusion reigned. Peasants fleeing from their homes filled the roads, getting in the way of bewildered troops retreating in panic before the relentless moving wall of Hitler's tanks. Russian morale was at an all-time low.

As the endless lines of tanks, trucks, and armored cars poured across the steppes, small guerrilla bands of partisans did what they could to harass and delay the advance. They blew up bridges; they sniped at ammunition caravans. Cossacks, wearing their red-and-blue-topped sheepskin hats and long black coats, appeared out of nowhere—sometimes riding their shaggy ponies, sometimes on foot—attacked, and vanished.

On one occasion, a German supply line nine miles long was approaching a fork in the road near the village of Beketovka. The Germans had posted a five-man advance guard to see that the column took the right fork. A dozen or so partisans surprised the guards and shot them all. Then they swiftly moved a shed across the road the Germans should have taken. When the vehicles came up, they followed the wrong fork, which led them off into a cow path. There they milled about, a perfect target for snipers. The resulting turmoil caused a three-day delay.

Russian soldiers take positions on the front southwest of Stalingrad.

Wherever there was opposition or sabotage, the Germans retaliated, standing villagers up before firing squads or conducting wholesale hangings in the square. But these incidents served only to goad the peasants to further attacks and to further self-sacrifice.

The Russian armies continued to fall back. Fighting mostly with artillery, they fired mainly to cover their retreat. They seldom threw their own tanks into action, evidently not wanting to take chances with the few that they had. The absence of any strong opposition and the haste of the Russian withdrawal confirmed for Hitler the belief that his foe must be flabby, lacking both the will and the means to fight.

"The Bear Won't Let Me"

There were only two places between Hitler's forces and Stalingrad where the Russians seemed to have any chance of stopping, even temporarily, the headlong dash—the banks of two rivers, the Don and the Volga. First in the armies' path lay the Don, curling like a snake down through the steppes. To the east of the Don lay the wider and more strategic Volga.

There stood Stalingrad. It was not until the citizens learned that the Germans had reached the Don at a bend near Kotelnikovo and had established bridgeheads to get the troops across that they really understood the immediacy of the threat. On July 25, at this bend of the Don, the Germans first came up against a man who was later to play a lion's role in the defense of Stalingrad as head of the 62nd Army, but who was now temporarily head of the 64th Army—Vasili I. Chuikov. For the first time in the campaign, Russian soldiers put up a real fight. But after two days the Germans broke through again and continued their lunge forward.

In spite of the fact that the Russian forces were being badly overrun, one Russian general kept sending in glowing reports that a large German force was about to be entrapped.

Refugees leaving the city on the Volga in the wake of enemy bombing

Chuikov remarked dryly, "It was like the story of the man who said he had caught a bear. 'Well, bring him along.' 'I can't. The bear won't let me.'"

Chuikov organized a defense line at the Axai River, a tributary of the Don. Here he held the Germans in check for a week. Then he was forced back north to the Myshkova River. Now he was only about forty miles south of Stalingrad. But the Russians were fighting at last with desperation. Some of them tied grenades around their waists and flung themselves under the treads of advancing German tanks. It didn't matter that they blew themselves up, so long as they destroyed the tanks.

Stalingrad, alerted to the impending danger, began to prepare to withstand assault.

Some of the very old and the very young were evacuated east across the Volga. But most preferred to stay where they were. Families did not want to be split up; many old-timers refused to leave their homes. All able-bodied civilians between fifteen and fifty-five were organized into brigades, taking orders from their own leaders, who worked closely with military personnel. Besides turning out tanks in the great Tractor Plant, they also started digging an antitank trench, a tremendous undertaking. When finished, it was to stretch for twenty-five miles along the western perimeter of the city.

By the middle of August, two separate German forces were approaching Stalingrad. The 4th Panzer Army was on its way from the tip of the Don bend in the south, and the 6th Army was closing in from the northwest.

Terror from the Sky

For the people of Stalingrad, the day of August 23 was as catastrophic as a day could be. They had no air-raid warning system, no inkling of the disaster that was about to occur.

At daybreak, just as they were stirring from their sleep, they heard the drone of German planes overhead. Almost before they had time to ask what was happening, the bombs started to fall. The next sound they heard was the whistle and boom of the bombs going off. They ran outside into an inferno of flame and thunder, with walls collapsing all around them. If they had time they dived for the cellars. When there was a direct hit, they were either blasted to bits or incinerated before they had a chance to flee.

By nightfall, when the last wave of attacking planes droned off into the distance, some 40,000 civilians lay dead.

The survivors' first act was to dismantle the precious factories and start moving machinery across the Volga. When word of this reached Stalin, the Premier was furious. It is reported that he got the leaders on the telephone and said, "So you've got the evacuation fever too, eh? Well, stop it immediately. Stalingrad must be held at any price. Our soldiers are more likely to fight for a live town than for an empty town. Even if it costs us half a dozen factories, it'll be worth it."

Stalin's words had an electrifying effect. The evacuation halted. In the Tractor Plant, production resumed. Two hundred new tanks were turned out during the month of September. Night after night, tanks that had been built at the factory under enemy fire returned smoking from the battle lines to be put in shape for the next day's combat. The mechanics who had built them waited to do repairs. The tanks were coming home.

On the hills were huge oil-storage tanks that had exploded into flames. The burning oil slowly seeped downhill, then spread out over the Volga, making it look as if the very river were on fire. The wooden houses in the city's residential section blazed like so much kindling; other houses made of brick and stone, the buildings, and some of the factory walls, collapsed into piles of rubble. Here and there, blackened chimneys remained standing.

Mechanics repairing a Russian tank in the bomb-gutted Tractor Plant

A civilian carries a treasured possession through a battered street.

The civilians now began to stream eastward in large numbers, even though they had to make the river crossing under a rain of bombs and machine-gun bullets. Ferries, barges, armored boats, and even little fishing boats were hurried into service to get civilians out of the city.

General Chuikov has movingly described the plight of the homeless people of Stalingrad as follows: "As we drew closer [to a pier on the Volga] many wounded were being carried out of trenches, bomb-craters and shelters. There were also many people with bundles and suitcases who had been hiding from German bombs and shells. When they saw the ferry arriving they rushed to the pier, with the one desire of getting away to the other side of the river, away from their wrecked houses, away from a city that had become a hell. Their eyes were grim and there were trickles of tears running through the dust and soot on their grimy faces. The children, suffering from thirst and hunger, were not crying, but simply whining, and stretching out their little arms to the water of the Volga."

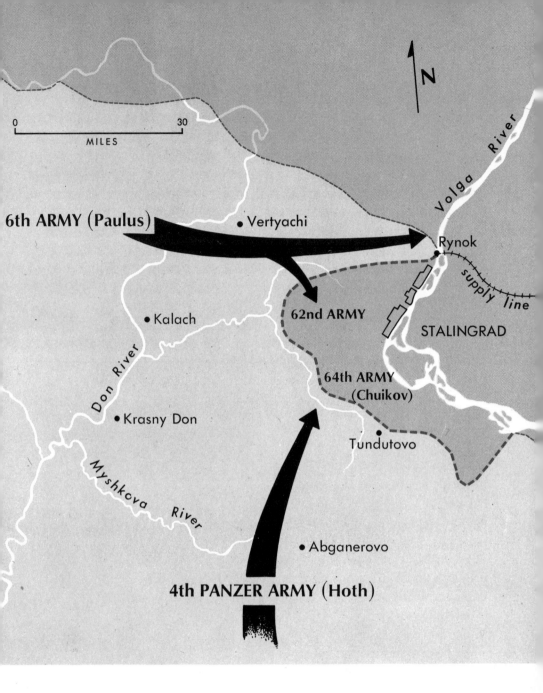

Situation August 31, 1942

front line : ━ ━ ━ ━ ━ ━

Considering the suddenness of the attack, there was, surprisingly, no panic—just bewilderment and confusion. The regular telephone service had been knocked out almost immediately. Fortunately, there was an auxiliary system set up between administrative headquarters, so that some communication was possible. The civilian population reported to their own headquarters, where they were given their armbands and instructions. They would not be caught off guard a second time.

Der Fueher had confidently expected that his thunderclap blow from the air, coupled with his panzer attack, would knock the city out completely and render it helpless.

Quite the contrary.

The very thoroughness of the air attack turned the city into a kind of fortress—a fortress that could be defended. The brick and rubble formed a protective cover against both machine-gun fire and falling bombs. There was little left to burn. In the cellars beneath the debris, both soldiers and civilians could go on living—and fighting.

The Russians immediately improvised a network of strongpoints—a grain elevator, a railroad station, a factory, or a department store—that could protect each surrounding area with defensive fire in all directions.

Every day German planes continued to crisscross the city. Meanwhile, the defending forces—the 62nd and 64th Armies—were still some miles away. They were retreating rapidly into Stalingrad. But, as before on the steppes, they found the roads choked with refugees, often pushing carts piled high with their household goods.

". . . Hold the City or Die"

On September 4, units of Hoth's 4th Panzer Army, driving up from Abganerovo, had reached the Volga at the southern suburb of Krasnoarmeisk, splitting the 64th Army. By September 10, other units had reached the Volga at Kuporosnoye, also south of the city. In doing so, they had driven a wedge between the 62nd and 64th Armies—the 62nd was caught within Stalingrad, while the 64th was cut off outside.

On that same day, the War Council issued an order to the troops: "The enemy must be smashed at Stalingrad."

In that command the Red Army and the citizens of Stalingrad seemed to find courage for renewed resistance despite the kind of conditions they were enduring—the terror of the daily bombings, the looming shortage of both food and ammunition.

"The giant sounds of war are cramped in the city, they scramble from stone to stone, they swell up, they grow by bumping against walls and then suddenly rush at us humans with a roar which knocks you unconscious, so that you lie for a while motionless, your face buried in the stones." So wrote Eugene Krieger in *Street in Stalingrad*.

Two days later Vasili Chuikov was made general of the 62nd Army and entrusted with the defense of the city. In March of that year, Chuikov had been recalled from Chungking, China, where he had been serving as military adviser to Generalissimo Chiang Kai-shek in his fight against the Japanese. Chuikov, then forty-four, was stolid, stocky, unshakable; he displayed a mouthful of gold teeth when he smiled. A professional soldier, he was considered by the Russians to be one of the Red Army's ablest commanders. He had no experience as yet, however, with the German style of mechanized warfare. Upon receiving the appointment, General Chuikov sent this message to Nikita Khrushchev of the War Council and to the commander of the Stalingrad front: "We shall either hold the city or die."

General Chuikov proceeded to move in with the 62nd. Near the center of Stalingrad was a piece of ground about a hundred yards high called Mamayev Kurgan (Hill), which was topped by a cemetery. It was to become famous during the siege as the most fought-for position in Stalingrad, partly because it marked the dividing line between the factory district to the north and the business area to the south, but mostly because it was the city's highest point.

On September 12, General Chuikov, digging in for Stalingrad's defense, established his command post at the top of Mamayev Hill.

Nineteen Tanks Hold the Line

The Germans again launched a terrifying attack on the following day. In the first wave of bombing and shelling, General Chuikov found, in his exposed position at the top of the hill, that the lines of his field telephone were repeatedly being broken; he could no longer command his troops.

A trying situation occurred, which General Chuikov describes, with an element of bitter humor, in his book *The Battle for Stalingrad:* "During the whole day of the 13th, none of us, either officer or soldier, had had anything to eat. Our lunch was

General Vasili Chuikov
(A post-war photograph)

being cooked in a small house on the side of a hill, but an enemy bomb destroyed both the kitchen and our lunch. Our cook tried to cook our dinner in a field kitchen, but this was also smashed by a direct hit. Our cook wasn't going to waste any more food on us, so we stayed hungry all day."

Chuikov moved to a new command post in a sheltered bunker in Tsaritsa Ravine. The new post was farther to the south—between two railroad stations, near the Volga and enemy lines.

At noon, defenders of downtown Stalingrad heard an omi-

Russians shoot their way to a Nazi strongpoint near Central Station.

nous rumble. German armored columns had penetrated to the heart of the city. Tanks led the way, shooting as they came. Hard behind them followed the motorized infantry. These columns headed for the key point of Central Station. Except for piles of debris in the streets, they found their progress almost unimpeded. Scouts reported to General Chuikov in his bunker that several German tanks were no more than eight hundred yards away at that very instant.

Chuikov had been keeping nineteen fresh tanks of his own— the last he had—in reserve for dire emergency.

The emergency had come.

At about this time, Nazi soldiers, having poured victoriously into the city, concluded that Stalingrad had fallen.

Chuikov describes the moment this way: "The Nazis were now apparently convinced that the fate of Stalingrad was sealed, and they hurried towards the Volga. . . . Our soldiers—snipers, anti-tank gunners, artillerymen—lying in wait in houses, cellars and firing-points, could watch the drunken Nazis jumping off the trucks, playing mouth organs, bellowing and dancing on the pavements."

The Russians, however, didn't know they were defeated. Now they blasted away at point-blank range, killing Nazis by the hundreds. But thousands more kept coming into the city.

That night Chuikov ordered his handful of tanks to counter-attack. He reminded his tank commanders of orders previously issued: "Whatever you meet, never turn back. If your tank is damaged, go on firing from a standstill. If you are left alone, fight on alone. That clear?"

The battle was particularly hot around Central Station, which changed hands several times during the night. When the Germans occupied the waiting rooms, Russian snipers and machine gunners pinned them down from positions in sheds and from charred, bombed-out railway carriages on the sidings.

The German tide had been checked—but for how long?

"Rat War" in the Cellars

One evening, a dust-covered figure suddenly appeared at Chuikov's command post. This was Major General Alexander Ilyich Rodimtsev, commander of the crack 2nd Guards Rifles Division, who had been fighting in the north. To Chuikov's surprise, Rodimtsev reported that his division, numbering 10,000 men, was almost intact and was available, although short of arms and ammunition.

But there remained a problem. Rodimtsev's men were still to the north, with a strong German force between their lines and Chuikov's men. Chuikov was fighting with the remnants of the seven or eight divisions that had been retreating for the last six weeks. Their numbers had been decimated, and the men were weary. At this critical moment, Rodimtsev's fresh troops could be all-important to the defenders of Stalingrad, whose meager strength was fast ebbing away.

A bold plan for an elaborate ferrying campaign was worked out. The Rodimtsev division crossed the Volga to the east bank, then moved down to a point opposite the center of the city. From there they were ferried across into the city. They finally effected a landing just near the foot of Mamayev Hill.

All this was going on while German tanks were fighting in the streets of Stalingrad.

Take the Hill!

By the time Rodimtsev's forces landed, the Germans had captured Mamayev Hill. This gave them an observation post from which they could direct the dive bombing of strongpoints throughout the city.

Chuikov could not allow the Germans to hold this advantage. He issued these orders to Rodimtsev: Two regiments are to clear the enemy from the center of the city; one is to storm Mamayev Hill and retake it from the Germans.

Almost from the moment they landed, on the evening of September 14, Rodimtsev's men went into action. The hill was stormed in a heroic battle.

All during the day of the fifteenth, the conflict surged. Again and again Rodimtsev's men swarmed up the slopes into the face of German machine-gun fire. Again and again they were driven back with terrible losses. The men who remained alive returned

Four Russian infantrymen leap to shore on the east bank of the Volga.

to the attack. Five times the top of the hill passed from one side to the other throughout the day and night.

But as the sun rose on the morning of the sixteenth, Mamayev Hill was firmly in Russian hands.

They had paid dearly for the prize. Rodmitsev's regiment was almost wiped out. His men had died by the hundreds in the assault. Although other units displayed equal bravery and self-sacrifice in later engagements, none earned the fame of Rodimtsev's soldiers.

In the city below, things were not going so well for the Russians. The Germans still held the Central Station and were bringing up more and more reinforcements to strengthen their position.

But the strongpoints were holding. The Russian fighters were also being reinforced. Snipers and antitank gunners firing from behind brick walls kept the Nazis from extending their gains.

By September 16, with Mamayev Hill won again and the Germans checked for the moment at least, the defenders of Stalingrad began to feel that their cause was not altogether hopeless.

Ilya Ehrenburg, the well-known Russian writer, summed up the Russian feeling of horror at the destruction and death brought on them by the Germans, mingled with the hope of eventual victory: "Of course, there are in this [German] army a few thinking and feeling individuals, but they are alone among millions; they are ladybirds sitting on the back of a mad elephant. We have no time and no desire to bother about ladybirds. We must shoot the mad elephant."

From that day until November 19, the Battle of Stalingrad stormed unabatedly with only the briefest of lulls, which either were brought on by bad weather or occurred as the Germans regrouped their forces for another *Blitz* attack.

RIGHT: *In Fortress Stalingrad—ladders of stone for men of iron will*

Boats on the Volga

Both attackers and defenders had settled into their underground positions, where for weeks they were to live like moles. What kept the city going—besides unquenchable courage—was the supply line along the Volga.

Here it was revealed that the Russians had a positive genius for camouflage, the art of disguising equipment and supply dumps so that the enemy does not recognize them. German planes flying over the Volga by day would see along the banks a perfectly natural thicket of willows. But as night fell, the branches would be removed, and out would come a fast, streamlined speedboat, her crew ready to take her across the river once more.

Here is an incident typical of many in the hazardous undertaking: A Lieutenant Leonov went with his boat to assist another one night. Afterward he was ordered to ferry thirty tommy gunners and six tons of ammunition over the Volga. On the way across, his own boat went aground on a sunken hulk.

"The night protected the crew from danger but the dawn was near," wrote Krieger. "The propeller churned furiously but could not get her off. The men jumped into the icy water which came up to their necks and tried to push her off by main force, but soon had to give up. A few men struggled to the bank with a rope and tried to haul her off, intending to unload her near the bank. . . . The men hauled until their hands were raw—but the boat did not budge. The sunken barge held her as in a vise.

"Time was going by, dawn was approaching and with it the fire of the enemy. Counting the minutes, the crew scrambled ashore, found an old warped and sunken hulk, launched her . . . and with this wreck and a raft improvised out of a few logs, they landed the six tons of precious ammunition and the 30 tommy gunners, who immediately went off to join in the fighting. At daybreak the lightened boat was refloated under her own power at the very moment when another vessel came to her rescue from their base."

Fighting in the Streets

The daytime belonged to the Germans, who blasted the city with bombs and artillery fire. But at night they walked softly and carefully, for it was then that the Russians came out from their ratholes and attacked wherever they saw a German uniform. This was the beginning of what the invaders called the *Rattenkrieg* ("Rat War").

Each fresh German tank attack won a few yards. But for the time being at least, they made no gains of importance.

Most of the hand-to-hand fighting took place in the flattened ruins of the workers' garden-city settlements at the north end of Stalingrad. Here a front line of sorts had developed. The opposing forces faced each other across a no-man's-land no more than a hand grenade's throw in width. It was this area that saw some of the most desperate close-quarters fighting of the siege.

Chuikov gives a vivid picture of this kind of warfare in his instructions for street fighting. Briefly, an attacking unit was composed of a storm group of six to eight men who were lightly armed with grenades, tommy guns, knives, and shovels. Once inside, they signaled the larger, or reinforcement, group, which then rushed in, took over old firing points and established new ones, thus preventing the Germans from aiding their people inside. The reinforcements were more heavily armed with anti-tank rifles and cannons, mortars, crowbars, explosive charges, and so on. There was a reserve group if needed.

Relating the instructions he gave to a novice in a shock group, Chuikov wrote: "There must be two of you to rush a house—you and a grenade. Both of you should be lightly dressed

—you, without your haversack, and the grenade without its shirt. This is how you rush a house: Let the grenade go in first and then you follow. Go through the whole house the same way: first the grenade, then you, yourself."

Chuikov brought his battle lines as close to the Germans as possible. He knew that if he got close enough, the Germans would not dare to bomb his positions for fear of hitting their own.

One of the first decisions of the Stalingrad defenders had been to move their artillery across to the east side of the river. Now the farsightedness of this move began to pay off. The Russians, who were by far the better marksmen with their artillery, began to bring the German positions under merciless bombardment, both from their heavy guns and from their *katyushas*. (The *katyusha* was a mortar, a kind of short, wide-mouthed cannon that fired a bomb rather than a shell. The Russians used

Russian riflemen fighting in the rubble on the outskirts of the city

Soviet soldiers charge across a bridge toward a German position.

katyushas with deadly effect, both in defending themselves and in later counterattacks.)

In this kind of fighting, individual prowess and courage became all-important.

"Towards the end of September," wrote Chuikov, "storm troops appeared in all regiments; these were small but strong groups as wily as a snake and irrepressible in action. The Germans rarely stood up against an attack by bullet and grenade backed by bayonet and dagger. Fighting went on for buildings and in buildings—for a cellar, for a room, for every corner in a corridor. Streets and squares were empty.

"Our commanders and men learned to crawl right up to enemy positions during enemy bombardments and bombing and by doing so avoid being killed. . . . We deliberately fought as close as possible."

The Duel

Outstanding among these storm groups were the snipers. In this kind of warfare, one man who was a dead shot with his rifle was the equal of a whole company of the enemy. A spontaneous competition developed among the Russian soldiers. They tried to outdo one another in the number of Germans each man accounted for. From this rivalry emerged a soldier named Vasili Zaitsev. An excellent shot, he also instructed others in marksmanship. One outstanding pupil, Viktor Medvedev, ultimately shot more than the three hundred Germans chalked up by Zaitsev.

Four Russians stalk a sniper near the Barricades Machinery Factory.

Russian snipers were becoming a real threat to the enemy. In fact, the Russians learned one day from a talkative prisoner that the Germans were sending their best man, a certain Major Koning, chief instructor of the Nazi sniper school in Berlin, to the Stalingrad front. Major Koning was under orders, so the prisoner said, to dispose of both Zaitsev and his pupil Medvedev personally.

Koning soon made his presence felt. Marksmanship among the Germans improved rapidly. Soon no Russian dared raise his head above a trench or a protecting wall.

Things reached a point where Zaitsev was given orders similar to those given the German major; he was to get rid of Koning—personally.

Out of this situation developed a gun duel of epic proportions.

In a certain trench where Zaitsev was stationed, he noticed that one rifle shot after another was being directed at him with uncomfortable accuracy. A number of crack Russian snipers were being put out of commission.

Just opposite the trench, the Germans held three protected positions. On the right was a burned-out tank; on the left, a pill-box. Directly in front was a sheet of iron lying on some bricks; it had been there so long that the Russians hardly paid any attention to it. But gradually they saw that the deadly shots were coming from right in front of them rather than from either side. Finally, after one shot, they saw a tiny puff of smoke drifting in the air above the sheet of iron. This left no doubt. The German marksman was behind it, evidently firing through a tiny slit.

Now the Russians resorted to a series of tricks. One man raised a helmet above the trench on the end of his bayonet. It drew a bullet. A few minutes later, they put up a mitten. Another bullet.

While this was going on, Zaitsev wormed his way around to a position from which he could look at the bricks and the sheet iron from one side.

At the next shot, he fired. A German helmet rolled out and down the bricks. Zaitsev had no doubt that the helmet was Koning's.

The duel was over.

Battle for the Factories

On September 27, the Germans concentrated on the factories for the first time. The attack was preceded by one of the worst

Russian workers ready for action near the Red October garden city

dive bombings yet. The Germans counted on their heavy supe-
riority in planes and tanks. From their artillery emplacements
on the other side of the river, the Russians launched a heavy
barrage of their own. The Germans suffered staggering losses,
but they picked their way through the Russian minefields and
penetrated almost two miles into the city.

Now the fighting centered around the three biggest factories
—the Tractor Plant, the Barricades Machinery Factory, and the
Red October Metallurgical Plant.

The Germans fought their way into the grounds and in some
places into the factories themselves, which now became the
battleground. Russians and Germans fired on one another at
close range from behind desks in the offices or from the wreckage of lathes and grinders in the workshops.

General Chuikov sent an urgent radio message to Khrushchev,
the member of the War Council entrusted with the defense of
Stalingrad, asking for reinforcements. Khrushchev replied
promptly that help would be forthcoming.

That night, while the fighting was going on in the factories,
two regiments of fresh troops, under General Fedor Nikandro-
vich Smekhotvorov, were ferried across the Volga and landed
to join the fighting in the Red October garden city.

In the next few days the situation went from bad to worse
for the Russians. The Germans again won the top of Mamayev
Hill. Rodimtsev's regiment, which had been almost wiped out,
was replaced by men from General N. F. Batyuk's division.
They hung on stubbornly to the northeastern slope, but by
October 9 the Germans had a firm grip on the entire hill, which
they were to hold for some time. It did not benefit them as much
as they had hoped, however, for their exposed position on the
area's highest point was a prime target for Russian artillerymen
outside the city.

At the foot of Mamayev Hill, Chuikov's forces were being
heavily battered. His men had their backs against the Volga

Russian soldiers are ferried across the Volga to join in the fighting.

They could not retreat. Minute by minute they were being squeezed into an ever-narrowing strip.

Then came a bad moment for Chuikov himself. German bombs scored a direct hit on some oil tanks directly above Tsaritsa Ravine, where he had his command headquarters. Rivers of flaming oil came pouring down the hillside, a moving blanket of flame.

"The staff at my command post were choking with heat and smoke," Chuikov recalls. "The fire of the flaming oil tanks was crawling down to our dugout. Every dive-bomber attack was killing people and putting our wireless sets out of action."

The headquarters staff managed to close the ports of their bunkers just ahead of the flaming flood. They survived somehow until the worst of the fire had passed.

"...Shells and Bombs from Morning till Night"

Despite repeated German mass assaults, the last week of September, 1942, found Stalingrad still holding out. But the fate of the city, and indeed of the whole Allied cause, still hung in the balance.

In North Africa, Rommel still had the upper hand over the British, who were throwing in everything they could spare in an all-out effort to stop him.

In the United States, planes, tanks, and guns at last, after months of retooling of the factories, were beginning to roll off the assembly lines in large numbers. Some were sent off at once for Russia via the Arctic route to Murmansk. But no one was very hopeful that enough of them would reach the receding Russian lines in time to be of much help.

Far behind the Russians' own lines, the factories were going full blast. But where were the tanks? They were certainly not obstructing the German advance in any numbers.

Bloody October

Every day throughout the first week of October, the Germans launched a new attack, trying first to get a foothold in the factory district and then to hang on to it. At last, on October

A Luftwaffe bomber

7, they succeeded. They gained and clung to a position in the ruins of the workers' settlement just behind the Tractor Plant. Elsewhere their efforts were futile. One building in the garden city just behind the Red October Plant changed hands five times.

Suddenly came an ominous lull; it began on the ninth and lasted through the thirteenth. The Russians could only wait and wonder what new move the Germans were plotting now. The defenders thought they must be realigning their forces for another blow.

Where would it fall?

"The 14th of October marked the beginning of a battle unequalled in its cruelty and ferocity through the whole of the Stalingrad fighting," wrote Chuikov. "Three infantry and two Panzer divisions were hurled at us along a five kilometer front [a little over three miles]. There were three thousand German air sorties [a sortie is one flight by one plane] that day. They bombed and stormed our troops without a moment's respite. The German guns and mortars showered on us shells and bombs from morning till night. It was a sunny day but owing to the smoke and soot visibility was reduced to 100 yards. Our dugouts were shaking and crumbling up like a house of cards. . . .

"The command and observation posts of regiments and divisions were being smashed by shells and bombs. At my army's command post 61 people were killed. The guards scarcely had time to dig the officers out of the smashed dugouts of the army H.Q. [headquarters]. The troops had to be directed by radio; transmitters had been set up on the other side of the Volga, and we communicated with them and they then passed on our orders to the fighting units on this side of the river."

At one point, Chuikov's headquarters was within three hundred yards of the advancing Germans. Two days later the Nazis mounted a fierce attack by picked machine gunners to try to capture General Chuikov and his headquarters staff. They failed, but only by a narrow margin.

Losses from the all-out offensive were staggering on both sides. Dozens of Der Fuehrer's tanks were put out of commission; hundreds of German dead covered the ground. But on the

Soviet tommy gunners advance around a smouldering German tank

Russian side, three out of every four of Zholudev's and Go-rishnyi's troops had been killed. After exhausting struggles, the Germans were in possession of the Tractor Plant itself. But around the Red October Plant and in the nearby garden city, the Russians still clung to every foot.

Early in October a division under command of Colonel L. N. Gurtiev appeared on the scene, having crossed the Volga at night. His troops were Siberians, doughty frontiersmen to begin with; they were battle-hardened veterans who had been fighting all the way on the retreat from the west. They were ordered to hold the Red October Plant, the chief target of the Germans. Upon arrival, Gurtiev's men found that the Germans had already captured the neighboring workers' settlement and had broken into the factory grounds. What was to prevent the Nazis from cutting right through to the Volga?

"Here was concentrated the entire diabolical arsenal of German militarism—super-heavy and flame-throwing tanks, six-barrelled mortars, armadas of dive-bombers fitted with screaming sirens, splinter bombs and demolition bombs," wrote Vassili Grossman, Russian war correspondent. "Here was concentrated German artillery, anything from small calibre anti-tank semi-automatics to heavy long-range guns. Here night was as light as day from the glares of fires and flares, and day as dark as night from the smoke of burning buildings and German smoke-screens."

But the Siberians hung on. Only a small force of Nazis got through to the outbuildings of the factory. All through that month the battle for the Red October Plant still raged. In one day Gurtiev's men were attacked twenty-three times. The factory changed hands repeatedly. It was subjected to 117 assaults. Still the Siberians could not be dislodged.

Not all the encounters were impromptu. Some of the actions were thoroughly prepared for in advance. A case in point was the taking of a strategic house in the center of the city by some

Colonel Gurtiev addresses troops before advancing into the city.

of Rodimtsev's men. Grossman described it in *Red Star*, the Communist newspaper, on October 27: "The plan for the storming of this house was highly elaborate, full of minute details. In the plan of the house every room that had a sniper or a machine gun was marked down accordingly. Every detail of the front stair and the back stair was marked. The house was stormed with the help of mortar crews, grenade-throwers, snipers, tommy-gunners, the regimental artillery and the heavy artillery on the other side of the Volga. Everything was closely coordinated through signals, rockets, radio and telephone."

Throughout the month, the Germans continued their heavy attacks. But these were concentrated on ever-narrowing sectors. It became clear to the Russians that the enemy was running out of steam. But the strength of the defenders was fast dwindling too.

By October 20, Chuikov was drawing on his forces behind the lines—shoemakers, blacksmiths, tailors, and storekeepers.

Women at War

As the ranks of the men grew thin, women came out of the caves and cellars, where they had been looking after their parents and children, to fill the empty places. They manned the searchlights, the radio and telephone communications systems, and the antiaircraft batteries. They served as nurses, orderlies, doctors.

General Chuikov pays them tribute: "They would stick to their guns and go on firing when bombs were exploding all around them, when it seemed impossible not merely to fire accurately, but even to stay with the guns. In the fire and smoke, amid bursting bombs, seemingly unaware of the columns of earth exploding into the air all about them, they stood their ground to the last."

A brigade made up entirely of women fought alongside the men in the Red October Plant. Their leader was killed in a hand-to-hand battle, but they fought on.

The stories of most of these heroic women have been lost in the debris of battle. One, which has been preserved in the archives of the Red Army, must stand for many. This is the last report by radio to the Army Signal Center by a girl named Nadya Klimenko: "There is no one left near the post. I am alone. Shells are bursting all around. . . . To the right I can see tanks moving with crosses painted on them, and there are infantrymen behind them. . . . It's already too late for me to leave. I should care if they shoot! I'll go on reporting just the same. Listen! There's a tank coming up to my post. . . . Two men are getting out of it. . . . They are looking around—I think they're officers. They're coming towards me. My heart's stopped beating with fear of what's going to happen. . . ."

And then—no more.

Camouflaged troops and horses cross a water barrier on pontoon rafts.

The Last Big German Offensive

During the fighting in the last ten days of the month, the Germans captured the Tractor Plant and the northwest part of the territory around the Red October Plant. At one point, between the Barricades Machinery Factory and the Red October Plant, they were within four hundred yards of the Volga. This brought the last Volga crossing, by which reinforcements were brought over, within machine-gun range. But the defenders threw up stone walls to protect the barges, and the ferrying continued.

General Paulus, commander of Germany's 6th Army, assured Hitler he would occupy Stalingrad by November 10. But that day found the Russians still entrenched along the Volga.

On November 9 the Russians learned that a group of German street-fighting specialists had landed at the three German-held

airports and had been hustled off to the center of the city to join the coming assault. Something big was in the wind. On November 11, perhaps in a last desperate effort to make good on his promise, even if a little late, Paulus launched one of his most formidable attacks. The full German might was again unleashed against the defenders.

The Red artillery and *katyushas* from across the Volga dropped a curtain of fire that the Germans could not penetrate. But ammunition was running low. Then, looking out over the Volga, the Russian gunners saw large white chunks floating on the broad black surface of the river.

Ice!

A few more weeks and the Volga would freeze over. But in the interim, the floating ice cakes would choke it, forcing the boats carrying shells, bullets, and food to go more slowly—or to stop altogether.

Once again the Germans rushed Mamayev Hill, now defended by General Batyuk's division. By noon of November 11, his 118th Guards Regiment, originally 250 strong, had only six men still able to fight. But the Russians threw in reinforcements, and the hill was held.

Just north of the hill, the Germans broke through to the Volga along a five-hundred-yard front, once more cutting Chuikov's 62nd Army in two. The isolated knots of defenders had to be supplied at night by small planes. But elsewhere the Russians did not yield. The Germans advanced their lines no more than a hundred yards closer to the Volga; even this slight gain cost them as many men as they had lost in advancing two thousand yards a few weeks before.

Fortunately for the defenders—although they did not know it at the time—they would have to withstand this kind of pounding for only eight more days.

LEFT: *Twisted steel makes an obstacle course of the Tractor Plant.*

The Allies Push Out

Elsewhere in the world the scales of war had begun to tip heavily against Hitler.

In North Africa, the British and troops from other Commonwealth countries finally met Rommel head on, at El Alamein, on October 23. In a gigantic tank duel that lasted several days, the Desert Fox was soundly beaten, the back of his Afrika Korps broken. By November 4, Rommel was in full retreat.

Then, on November 8, the news reached Hitler that the United States had entered the war in the Western Hemisphere, effecting a successful landing on the North African coast. This came as a shocking surprise, for the great task force of men, planes, and landing craft had been assembled off the coast of Gibraltar with the utmost secrecy.

And Der Fuehrer's generals had not yet been able to conquer Stalingrad.

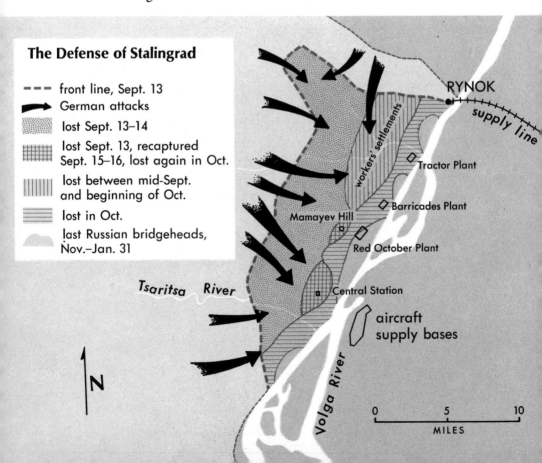

The Defense of Stalingrad

--- front line, Sept. 13
➤ German attacks
lost Sept. 13–14
lost Sept. 13, recaptured Sept. 15–16, lost again in Oct.
lost between mid-Sept. and beginning of Oct.
lost in Oct.
last Russian bridgeheads, Nov.–Jan. 31

RYNOK

supply line

workers' settlements

Tractor Plant

Barricades Plant

Mamayev Hill

Red October Plant

Tsaritsa River

Central Station

aircraft supply bases

Volga River

N

0   5   10
MILES

As the weeks went by and it still held out, the city named for Hitler's rival dictator became a kind of mocking symbol, goading him to fury by its resistance. He was determined to take Stalingrad no matter how much it cost in German lives.

New Sound of War

The chill winds of approaching winter now made the basement hideouts of the Stalingrad defenders more uncomfortable than ever. But as day after day went by and Paulus failed to repeat his thunderous assault of November 11, a feeling—barely perceptible at first—that they were going to win after all if they could just hold out began to seep through the Russian ranks.

The defenders didn't have much to go on. By November 14, the Germans were holding two strong positions on the banks of the Volga. But the assault seemed to be losing its momentum. The Nazis appeared to have neither the men nor the equipment to do any more than cling to the spots they already held. Both sides were becoming exhausted. From now on the siege of Stalingrad would be a war of endurance.

At four o'clock on the morning of the nineteenth, the battle-weary Russian soldiers and civilians, trying to snatch a few hours' sleep or stalking the enemy through the streets, strained their ears to catch a distant sound, so strange at that time of night, when all was quiet in the city. It was coming from a bend in the Don seventy-five miles to the northwest. Here one part of Hitler's large force, mainly troops of satellite countries, Rumania and Italy, was known to be encamped.

This time it was not German—but Russian—artillery beginning the predawn barrage. It could mean only one thing: the moment had arrived for which the defenders had waited so hopefully for so long.

From street fighter to street fighter, from bunker to bunker, the word was passed: "The counterattack has begun!"

Counterattack

After four hours of firing without pause, the artillery bombardment suddenly ceased. There followed a few moments of deadly stillness. Huddled in their shelters and foxholes to escape the shelling, the Nazi soldiers braced themselves.

Then, on the stroke of eight o'clock, the fog-shrouded tree trunks suddenly belched flame. Row after row of Russian tanks—fifty abreast—came clanking out of the Kremenskaya forest on the east bank of the Don, bearing down on the Rumanians. Every tank swarmed with infantrymen—"like ants on a lump of sugar." Submachine guns at the ready, hand grenades on their belts, they awaited the signal to leap down and storm the enemy positions. At the same time, the sky overhead was black with Russian planes.

For the first time, the Russians, under General Nikolai Vatutin, were attacking with vastly superior strength. They outnumbered the Rumanians three to one in men and four to one in tanks, trucks, and planes. The paint was still fresh on some of the tanks, which had only recently arrived from factories far behind the lines.

The great counteroffensive had been planned as far back as August by the Russian War Council, when the outlook appeared dark indeed. It represented the combined strategy of Premier

Josef Stalin, General Georgi Zhukov, and Chief of Staff A. M. Vasilievski.

By a shrewd stroke, the Russian strategists had picked a weak spot against which to deliver the heaviest blow. It was a sector held by the Rumanian 3rd Army, under Colonel General Dimitrescu. In Hitler's mind, this was the rear, and therefore he had not bothered to equip it with his strongest weapons of defense. The front was Stalingrad.

The Rumanians were an unknown quantity. Their government, one of Hitler's satellites, had sent them off to fight in Russia at Der Fuehrer's command. Mostly sturdy peasants, they hadn't much stomach for the job. Since Hitler didn't altogether trust them, the Rumanians had far fewer tanks and planes than the German divisions.

Throughout all the tense weeks when the defenders of Stalingrad were holding on by a thread, the Russian High Command was steadily moving great numbers of men and machines into striking positions northwest and southwest of the city. They

General Nikolai Vatutin

had refrained from opposing the German advance in force—although it must have taken iron nerve to delay—until they had the advantage of strength.

How had the Russians been able to carry out such a gigantic operation undetected by the Nazis?

There were three reasons for it: one, they clamped a rigid censorship on all mail; two, they had such great distances over which to move and such a wide choice of routes that Nazi reconnaissance planes could not possibly keep track of them all; three, they relied on their cleverness at camouflaging their equipment and positions.

In the north the many forests between Moscow and the Don made concealment not too difficult. But in the south General Andrei I. Eremenko had to move his forces for many miles over barren steppes. Tanks, trucks, and armored cars were in motion only at night. By day they were artfully hidden under thatches of grass or clumps of branches.

"Motor vehicles can hide like beetles in cracks and holes," wrote war correspondent Krieger. "They stick their noses into burrows dug by spades. They cling to the sides of ravines, are covered with thorn and thistle. Their drivers work like genuine gardeners or theatrical decorators. You seem to be walking through a desert, but the desert is full from end to end with panting, roaring motors."

The Cossacks Attack

At the same instant that the Russians were hurling their own modern might against the Rumanians, they launched another attack of an entirely different kind, typically Russian, equally fearsome. Fifty thousand Cossacks came hurtling out of the snow-shrouded landscape on horseback swinging their long sabers and shrieking their piercing, bloodcurdling battle cries.

The Rumanians were overwhelmed by these two sudden, dismaying onslaughts. Many fought bravely and died where they stood. Others fled.

Four Rumanian divisions were surrounded and, seeing the hopelessness of the situation, surrendered. When the smoke cleared away, the Russians took 30,000 prisoners, tearing a gaping hole in the German line.

Vatutin's forces swept on. Within three days he had penetrated the Nazi-held zone northwest of Stalingrad to an incredible distance of seventy miles along a wide front.

On the third day, Hitler rushed up neighboring German divisions to stem the advance. But there were not enough of them to prevail against Vatutin's victorious surge.

While Vatutin was working his way southeast, General Eremenko was coming up from the south with another strong force. On November 22, the two armies met at Kalach. At the same

Russians of Eremenko's and Vatutin's forces meet west of Stalingrad.

Cossacks in a headlong charge against the Rumanian 3rd Army

time, a third Russian army, under General Konstantin Rokossovsky, had broken through German lines and reached the Volga north of Stalingrad, neutralizing the German threat to Russian supply lines.

Now the three counterattacking armies could act in concert. By November 23, they had forged the first iron ring around the Germans.

Fortress Stalingrad

Some 330,000 German soldiers now found themselves encircled by Russians, caught in an irregular space no more than forty miles across in some places, as little as twenty miles from line to line in others. At the eastern perimeter of that ring was Stalingrad.

By this time an unseen ally had begun to favor the Russian cause—winter.

On the morning of November 19, the day of the great counterattack, a German command post northwest of the city recorded snow, a temperature of eighteen degrees, and winds of forty-two miles per hour.

The Russian soldiers were going into battle well equipped—not only with plenty of grenades and plenty of bullets for their submachine guns, but with white snow capes, warm coats, and boots.

The Germans, on the other hand, had only the thinnest of coats and ordinary shoes. Hitler, disregarding the suffering his troops had endured in the course of the disastrous winter retreat from Moscow in 1941, had failed to equip them for winter fighting.

Why?

Was it another one of his colossal misjudgments? Or had he done it deliberately, thinking it would goad his armies to finish the campaign before snow fell?

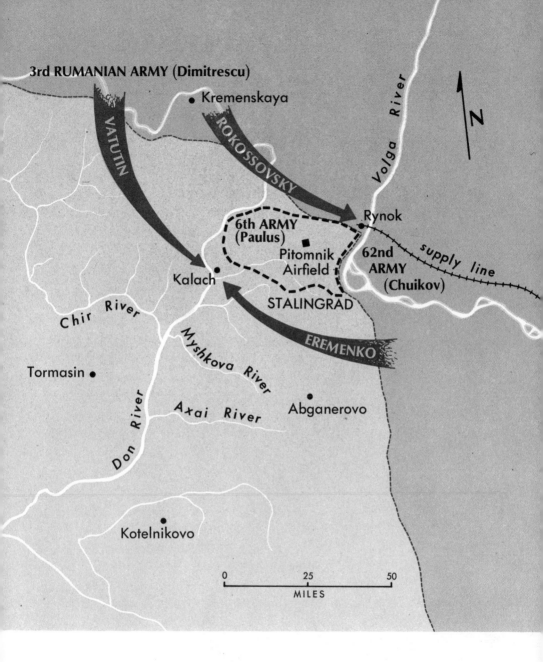

3rd RUMANIAN ARMY (Dimitrescu)

Kremenskaya

VATUTIN

ROKOSSOVSKY

Volga River

N

Rynok

6th ARMY
(Paulus)

Pitomnik
Airfield

62nd
ARMY
(Chuikov)

Kalach

STALINGRAD

supply line

Chir River

EREMENKO

Myshkova River

Tormasin

Axai River

Abganerovo

Don River

Kotelnikovo

| 0 | 25 | 50 |

MILES

Closing the Ring

- - - - - front line, November 23

---------- line of farthest German penetration

The cold and the succession of Russian victories were having a demoralizing effect on the Germans within the ring.

"The German prisoners I saw . . . wore ordinary coats and had blankets tied around their necks," wrote Henry Shapiro, an American correspondent for the United Press who followed in the wake of the Russian advance. "They had hardly any winter clothing at all. . . . The Germans seemed completely stunned, unable to understand what the devil had happened. . . .

"The steppe was a fantastic sight . . . strewn with dead horses and wrecked gun carriages, and tanks and guns, and no end of corpses, Rumanian and German. . . . Civilians were coming back to the villages, most of them wrecked. . . . Kalach was a shambles. Only one house was standing. . . .

A German soldier taken prisoner
at Stalingrad

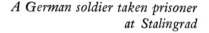

Russian riflemen in white snow capes crawl up to an enemy barricade.

"On my return journey I saw General Vatutin in a dilapidated schoolhouse at Serafimovich for a few minutes at four in the morning. . . . He was terribly tired; he had not had a proper sleep for at least a fortnight and kept rubbing his eyes and dozing off. For all that, he looked tough and determined and was highly optimistic."

Up to this point, it was mainly the armies of the satellite countries—Rumania and Hungary—that had given way. The German divisions themselves, although surrounded, were battle hardened and well equipped except for winter clothing and still presented a powerful striking force.

One chance remained for them—to mount a breakout through the rapidly tightening ring. For this purpose they chose a spot to the southwest of Stalingrad where Russian lines were weakest.

Paulus and the other German generals presented their plan to Hitler. But Der Fuehrer wouldn't hear of it. He refused to abandon Stalingrad, which by now had become an intensely emotional symbol to him.

Then, when all seemed hopeless, they found an unexpected champion in the person of General Kurt Zeitzler, recently appointed Chief of Staff.

Zeitzler had risen to power by being Hitler's yes-man. He had always been quick to do his Fuehrer's bidding. But the plight of the 6th Army was too desperate for even Zeitzler to accept without protest. On November 24, he presented the German generals' demands to Hitler at his headquarters in East Prussia in person, with his own endorsement.

For a few hours, Hitler appeared receptive to his Chief of Staff's pleadings. At his command post nine miles east of Stalingrad, General Paulus began preparations for the breakout. Then he sat by his radio waiting for the word that would set the machinery in motion.

He waited—and waited.

Late that afternoon, Hitler was also visited in his headquarters by fat, swaggering Reich Air Marshal Hermann Goering, a top Nazi and one of Hitler's cronies from his early days. Goering assured Der Fuehrer that the breakout would be quite unnecessary. Within the iron ring, three airfields were still working; the largest, Pitomnik, was at almost the center. Goering declared that the Luftwaffe, the Nazi air arm, would be able to supply the 6th Army with all the food, gasoline, and ammunition that it needed.

This was exactly what Hitler wanted to hear. He would not have to give up Stalingrad after all.

The radiotelephone at Paulus' command post crackled to life. But instead of getting the go-ahead he had been waiting for,

Paulus was asked to estimate how many tons of supplies he would have to have each day. Paulus asked for 700 tons; after haggling, Goering promised to deliver at least 550.

Hitler responded to the now critical situation with a typically theatrical gesture. He ordered Paulus to move his command post inside the city; gave the 6th Army a new name, Fortress Stalingrad; and commanded his generals to stand on the Volga.

Then, getting down to business, he ordered that all the units outside the ring be organized into a new fighting force, to be known as the Army of the Don, and put under the experienced panzer commander General Erich von Manstein. Tough, ruthless, and able, von Manstein had displayed in Hitler's conquest of the smaller countries of Europe a mastery of the *Blitzkrieg* technique similar to that of Rommel in North Africa.

Von Manstein's forces assembled some distance to the south and prepared to break into the ring and reinforce the Germans fighting in and around Stalingrad. At the same time, several other divisions—known as the Tormasin Group of the Army of the Don because they were assembled near that town—were to

General Erich von Manstein

break into the ring from the west and coordinate their attack with that of the von Manstein divisions coming up from the south.

The besieged Germans within the ring took heart when they heard that von Manstein was coming to their aid.

They needed heartening. Reich Air Marshal Goering's bland promises concerning the airlift weren't being carried out. At the most, the German transport planes were dropping only between 120 and 180 tons a day, and usually far less than that. All three airfields—Pitomnik, Gumrak, and a small one inside Stalingrad—were now under steady attack by Russian bombers and artillery.

Outside the Ring

Von Manstein put together an awesome fighting machine. It was to be led by the 4th Panzer Army, equipped with a large assemblage of tanks, variously estimated at between 250 and 600. His attack was to be known, appropriately enough, by the code name Operation Winter Gale. He was even lent one force from Army Group A, which was still fighting its way to Baku.

On December 12, von Manstein's columns started north. The speed of his movement caused the Russians grave concern. The crisis was not far off, for there were only two places where the Russians could hope to check him—at two rivers, first the Axai, then the Myshkova; and he was rapidly bearing down on the Axai.

Five Russian divisions opposed him. They engaged his forces at the Axai on December 15, but quickly withdrew before the superior firepower of his tanks. The Germans had no trouble crossing that first river, and they sped on toward the Myshkova.

Hitler's Tormasin Group had also started to move and was scheduled to pierce the ring and reach Stalingrad at about the same time that von Manstein did.

The Russians, however, had an ace in the hole—General Rodion Malinovsky, whose fresh troops, the 2nd Guards Army, were being held in reserve. But when Malinovsky got the order to move, he and his men were 125 miles to the east of von Manstein's advancing columns, on the other side of the Volga.

A Wall

Malinovsky's army at once began a forced march that was one of the great feats of the Stalingrad struggle. Through a blinding snowstorm and in below-zero temperatures, they moved to battle at the rate of twenty-five to thirty miles a day.

The Army of the Don had crossed the Axai River. Meeting with only light resistance, they were rapidly approaching the Myshkova.

At about this time, Malinovsky reached the Volga. The bitter weather that had impeded his march now became an asset. Instead of being choked with ice floes as it had been only a few days before, the Volga was now frozen over.

A column of tanks moves to Chuikov's rescue across the steppes.

As von Manstein moved swiftly northward along the south-western perimeter of the encircled German armies, General Vatutin was making deeper inroads into the enemy lines northwest of Stalingrad. He now had the same mastery of the air that the Germans had enjoyed in their first assaults on Stalingrad. In one day, Red planes flew 4,000 sorties.

Now Vatutin hit another soft spot, this time a sector held by the Italian 8th Army, comprised of five regular-army divisions and one division of Blackshirts. (The Blackshirts were the hand-picked fighting men of Italy's dictator, Il Duce, Benito Mussolini, who was a pale imitation of Der Fuehrer.) In this sector also were some remnants of the Rumanian 3rd Army and a force of Hungarians.

Again General Vatutin inflicted a smashing defeat on the Nazi armies. In the bloody engagement, 59,000 enemy soldiers were killed and 60,000 were taken prisoner.

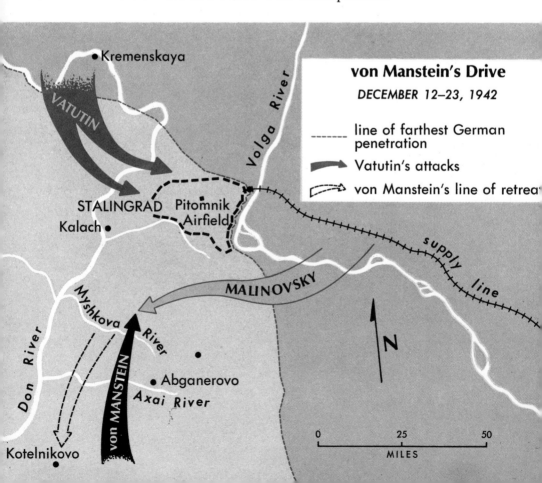

Hitler, alarmed by the gaping hole the Russians had torn in his lines, ordered the Tormasin Group of the Army of the Don moved northeast to stem the tide. This meant they could no longer help in the attack on Stalingrad.

Everything was going well, however, for von Manstein. His panzer divisions had crossed the Myshkova and had ground on for another ten miles. He was now within some thirty miles of Stalingrad. At night he and his men could see the red glow of the flares in the sky over the city that they hoped so soon to enter.

Convinced that he now had a chance of being successful, von Manstein took an unusual step. He issued an order to General Paulus—although Paulus was his equal in rank—stating that the latter was to fight his way out of the city to meet him.

Had Paulus acted promptly, history might have taken a different turn. But he waited for the order, which he knew was unauthorized, to be confirmed by Hitler. The confirmation never came. Paulus remained where he was.

Von Manstein returned to the attack. Suddenly, as he prepared to resume his advance, the road ahead swarmed with fresh Russian troops. He was up against a human wall; Malinovsky's forces had reached the scene and had moved into position to intercept him.

The Russian general had to give battle under a severe handicap. Because of the need to get there quickly, he had rationed his short supply of gasoline to his mobile artillery. These units, along with the infantry, had arrived ahead of his tanks. For the first few days, therefore, he held von Manstein's divisions at bay with his heavy guns and his foot soldiers alone. But on December 24, his tanks, now freshly fueled, caught up with his other units. For the first time, he was able to counterattack in force.

It now became clear that the Russians had had a definite strategy in mind in failing to resist von Manstein's advance from the Axai northward. The five original divisions that had opposed him on December 15 had simply melted away to either side of his advancing column instead of retreating ahead of him. From these positions they returned to the attack, harassing and disrupting the Germans' extended supply lines, as well as containing them within a narrow corridor so that they could not attack on a wide front.

What followed was nothing less than a rout. Malinovsky's 2nd Guards Army, with the help and support of the five other Russian divisions, drove von Manstein's panzers back across the

The road to Stalingrad was a dead end for many Nazi troops like these.

Myshkova, back across the Axai, back beyond Kotelnikovo, and even farther—pursuing the fleeing Germans far, far to the south.

All the hopes of the 6th Army troops that von Manstein would break in to come to their aid vanished.

Russian Offensive in Stalingrad

Within Stalingrad itself, the nature of the fighting was completely reversed. The War Council abruptly changed its directives. The order of the day was to root the last Germans out of the cellars and drive them from the city. Attacks from without

had subsided. The Nazi airlift was practically nonexistent now that Hitler could no longer replace the planes that had been shot down. Small groups of Germans, their ammunition rationed, huddled in their hideouts and fired only when fired upon.

"Clinging on to the factory buildings, the Germans are still hoping to keep the positions they previously captured and are defending themselves stubbornly," wrote war correspondent Vysokoostrovsky in *Red Star* on December 18. "Through open spaces, through the garden cities of the Workers' Settlements, through the platforms and workshops of the shattered factory buildings the front-line positions wind their way, forming a curious ribbon.

"The trenches on the two sides of the front almost touch each other at some points; buildings and remnants of buildings are wrapped in barbed wire, which also crosses streets and paths. Anyone little acquainted with the set-up would find it difficult to say what's what. The Germans have built here a hard defense line with substantial depth; here is a solid system of fortifications along the whole length of the front line; here are several rows of barbed wire, pillboxes, wood-and-earth works, mined areas, buildings turned into strong points.

"We also live mostly underground, and secret passages to the German positions are dug by our reconnaissance parties, who then blow up some of these positions from below. Then, over the wreckage thus formed, our infantry break through into the depth of the enemy lines. . . . The gaps thus formed enable our men to undertake more active operations on a larger scale and step by step the enemy defenses are being broken up."

Now the fighting often took the form of a war of wits as well as a war of cold nerves and cold steel. In the stalemate, Russians and Germans alike resorted to tricks and guile. The Germans masqueraded as Russians, wearing caps and uniforms they had stolen from the dead. They dressed up as women. The Russians did likewise.

A lieutenant with thirteen soldiers found his group entrenched opposite a German battery with particularly accurate aim. Whenever the Russians showed their heads, they were shot at. The Germans were strongly protected. The lieutenant saw no chance of blasting the battery out. Then, at his wit's end, he had an inspiration. Gathering his men about him, he ordered them to rattle their arms to make a clatter and then to cheer at the top of their voices.

The Germans, thinking the Russians must have received heavy reinforcements, shrank behind their cover. The Russians charged; their morale already shattered, the Germans fled.

Once-proud men of Paulus'
once-proud 6th Army

The battle of supplies had also shifted in favor of the Russians. The Volga, frozen over, was no longer an obstacle but a road. The Red Army, in control of the air, could drop food and ammunition by parachute to defenders who were fighting in isolation. The Germans, on the other hand, could no longer supply their troops inside Stalingrad by airlift. Both within the city and in the larger encirclement, Nazi soldiers were living mostly on horsemeat. When the horsemeat ran out, they ate dogs and cats and even rats.

"Those Germans who, in September, broke into houses and danced to the loud music of mouth organs, and who drove about at night with their headlights full on, and who, in broad daylight, would bring up their shells in lorries—the Germans are now hiding among the stone ruins," wrote *Red Star* correspondent Grossman.

"Now there is no sun for them. They are rationed to twenty-five or thirty rounds a day and they are to fire only when attacked. Their food ration is four ounces of bread a day and a little horseflesh. There, like savages grown over with wool, they sit in their stone caves, gnawing at a horse's bone. . . . Here in the dark, cold ruins of the city they have destroyed, they will meet with vengeance; they will meet it under the cruel stars of the Russian winter night."

In a large labyrinth of bunkers beneath the black and broken walls of Univermag Department Store, General Paulus operated his command post unknown to the Russians. Here he received his orders directly from Hitler.

From this post he now dispatched a command, hoping it would reach his troops still fighting in the iron ring being forged ever tighter around them.

"Stand fast! Stalingrad will be held!"

The order was ironic, for by now there was hardly a chance.

LEFT: *Two citizens of Stalingrad await enemy fire across factory ruins.*

The common soldier was disillusioned with his officers; the officers felt betrayed by the division commanders. Who was responsible? How had it all happened? No one seemed to know.

When an officer asked Paulus why he didn't defy Hitler and try to fight his way out on his own while there was still time, the German general revealed his point of view by replying, "It is not up to a soldier to judge; his only concern is discipline."

Within the ring, outside Stalingrad, the great German war machine was disintegrating. There was no longer any clear chain of command. Regiments were separated from their divisions, companies from their regiments, men from their companies.

The German soldier became an individual again instead of a cog in the juggernaut of war, a human being concerned only with trying to stay alive. And the odds were heavily against him. Many had frozen feet. When they went untreated, gangrene set in. The lucky ones got to a base hospital, where their legs were amputated. Others died by the roadside. Still others reached medical receiving centers only to find them abandoned, the doctors gone.

Nearly everyone was hungry. Supplies weren't being dropped in enough quantity to help much. The countryside had been picked clean. The best they could hope for was a little thin horsemeat soup. A bag of frozen potatoes was a luxury.

Pitomnik Airfield was the magnet. Whatever airdrops still got through fell there. Word went around that a few Junkers, homeward bound, were taking wounded. Soldiers walked all night to get to Pitomnik, where they bribed, lied, schemed, and fought each other for a place on a plane. Some drifted toward Stalingrad, hoping to find there some semblance of orderly defense.

And the thunder of guns grew ever closer as Vatutin and Rokossovsky tightened the noose, forcing the Germans into an ever-shrinking cul-de-sac. The 6th Army was now doomed.

Hitler's
Götterdämmerung

On the morning of January 8, 1943, three young Russian officers riding in a jeep and bearing a white flag crossed over into the German lines just north of Stalingrad. They were bringing an ultimatum from General Voronov, "representative of the general headquarters of the Supreme Command of the Red Army," and General Konstantin Rokossovsky demanding that Paulus and the 6th Army surrender.

The ultimatum ended: "The Red Army and Air Force will be compelled to wipe out the surrounded German troops. You will be responsible for their annihilation."

Paulus immediately got in touch with Hitler by radio. He asked that he be given the freedom to decide for himself whether to surrender or to keep on fighting.

A brief truce followed while Paulus waited for word from Der Fuehrer. Red Army soldiers went over to the German lines and pleaded with their enemies to give themselves up.

At last, word came from Hitler. He refused to give Paulus a free hand. He ordered him to fight on.

Two days later, on all fronts, the Russians broke the quiet with an artillery blast from 7,000 guns.

By early January the Russians had reduced the diameter of the ring in which 330,000 Nazi soldiers were entrapped to less than half of what it had been on the day of Vatutin's first attack. But the Germans, who had had time to dig in and set up concrete pillboxes, firing posts, and gun emplacements, were still capable of putting up a hard fight.

Russian artillerymen all around the edge of the ring had them well within range now and pounded them without letup. Red Army supply lines remained unbroken; shells and mortar bombs kept coming up in a never-ending flow.

Gasoline for the tanks and planes kept coming too. Army Group A had been halted within sixty miles of the coveted Baku oil fields, at a point where the Russians had taken advantage of the foothills to put up stiff resistance. Since there was no Stalingrad in the Caucasus to madden him, Hitler, on January 2, ordered Army Group A to withdraw. It was a stinging setback.

On that same day, the Red Army moved in and occupied Pitomnik Airfield, choking off the last of the German airdrops.

On January 17, the Russians repeated their demand to Paulus that he surrender. He did not reply.

General Konstantin Rokossovsky

Russian heavy artillery is zeroed in on the 6th Army inside Stalingrad.

By the time Paulus received the second ultimatum, he must have known that Hitler's orders to hang on to Stalingrad, to "fight to the last bullet," were the illusions of a madman and could result only in the needless slaughter of thousands of Paulus' soldiers.

A general, by the nature of his profession, must be a man of detachment. But one of the few deep feelings he can permit himself is concern for the men under his command. Paulus was such a general. Yet he was so conditioned by his life in the German war machine that he could only follow orders blindly —even though, from a military as well as a moral standpoint, he must have known them to be fatally wrong.

Even as Paulus rejected the second ultimatum by his silence, knots of German soldiers, broken men, the tattered shreds of his once-proud 6th Army, were plodding or limping east into Stalingrad along the route the retreating Russians had taken only a few weeks before.

Paulus' adversary, General Chuikov, was also still within Stalingrad, directing the 62nd Army from his command post. On January 26, Russian forces coming from the north and west entered the city, giving his garrison real strength.

A last burst of hand-to-hand fighting eddied through the streets. It continued for five days.

A Lieutenant Captures a General

From three German prisoners, the Russians learned one day that General Paulus himself had his command post in Stalingrad —underneath the Univermag.

By January 31, the Russians were in possession of the square where the department store was located. They began a systematic attack, first shelling what was left of the walls, then moving in and fighting from room to room with flamethrowers, ferreting out the last remaining Germans.

In East Prussia, Hitler and his aides sat around the radio listening to the grim message from Paulus' headquarters: "Our soldiers are deserting. . . . They are scarcely fighting any more. . . . It is useless to command them. . . ."

A few moments later: "The Russians are at the door of the bunker. . . . *We are destroying the command post.* . . ."

This announcement was repeated three times. After that came the call letters: "CL . . . CL . . . CL . . . ," which meant, in the international radio code, "This station is signing off." The hour was 5:45 P.M.

Then—silence.

The Russians, closing in for the kill, saw a man in a German officer's uniform appear in the entrance to the underground command post.

He was spotted by a young lieutenant, Fyodor Yelchenko, who was leading a small detail in the mopping-up operation. The German officer identified himself as Major General Raske, personal aide to General Paulus.

Yes, Paulus was inside. Paulus would be willing to talk if Yelchenko could produce someone of a rank equal to Paulus' own.

The young lieutenant laughed. He told Raske that all the members of the Red Army High Command were somewhat occupied at the moment. Then, taking three or four of his men with him and proceeding warily lest he be walking into a trap, Lieutenant Yelchenko entered the bunker.

"It was packed with soldiers," Yelchenko recalled later in an interview with Alexander Werth, British correspondent and historian of the Russian war effort. "They were dirty and hungry and they stank. And did they look scared! They all fled down here to get away from the mortar fire."

German prisoners of war straggle dejectedly into the heart of the city.

After some conversation, Yelchenko was conducted into an inner room, where a tall, lean man lay stretched out on an iron bed, gaunt, unshaven, staring into space, motionless except for a slight twitch in his cheek. This wreck of a man was General Paulus. He refused to say anything. He stared blankly into space. Here was the final ignominy.

The day before, when the fate of the 6th Army was all but sealed, Hitler, by radio, had elevated Paulus to the rank of Field Marshal. Why Hitler did this remains a mystery. Perhaps he thought that a man bearing the proud title of Field Marshal would indeed fight on to the last bullet as Der Fuehrer had ordered him to do—and possibly, if cornered, would use that last bullet to take his own life. Hitler, deprived of victory, would then at least have a conspicuous example of self-sacrifice that he could cite as typical of German heroism.

But things did not work out that way. Paulus, alive, was captured by a mere young lieutenant.

Raske held out for one last stipulation: that a staff car be sent to conduct Paulus personally to General Rokossovsky. The request was granted.

The officers and men of the 6th Army, once they heard that their commander had surrendered, gave themselves up en masse.

The Last Pocket

In the first official communiqué after the surrender, the Russians announced that they had taken 91,000 prisoners, including 24 generals and 2,500 other officers of lesser rank. They had also seized 750 planes, 1,550 tanks, 480 armored cars, 8,000 guns and mortars, 61,000 trucks, and great quantities of other equipment.

The Russians estimated that 140,000 Nazis either had been killed in the fighting or had died from untended wounds, disease, starvation, or exposure.

February 2, 1943—the Soviet victory banner is unfurled in Stalingrad.

A highly organized, superlatively equipped fighting force of 330,000 men was completely broken. The Russians had inflicted on Hitler the most crushing defeat ever suffered by a German army. One of the most decisive victories in military history had been won at Stalingrad.

Hitler could not keep the grim news from the German people. He decreed four days of mourning, closing all theaters, movie houses, and places of entertainment. The communiqué admitting the surrender was played over and over again on the Nazi radio, always preceded by a roll of drums and followed by the second movement of Beethoven's Fifth Symphony.

In the northern section of Stalingrad, one pocket of resisting Germans still fought on. They had not heard the news of surrender. Only when the Russians dropped photographs showing Paulus with General Rokossovsky did they finally give up, on February 2.

In his Wolf's Lair, Hitler is reported to have been enraged that Paulus had surrendered alive. He swore that he would never appoint another Field Marshal.

While soldiers of the Red Army moved over the steppes in search of prisoners and abandoned guns, men and women emerged from the caves and cellars beneath the ruins, blinking into the wan February sunshine of Stalingrad. Out of habit they still scanned the sky, instinctively listening for the drone of approaching Nazi bombers. Citizens trickled back to the ruins of what had once been their homes, their faces streaming with tears at what they saw.

One afternoon a few days later, a squadron of Russian Stormovik planes came up over the city in triumphal parade. As they flew they formed the five-pointed Red Star, national emblem of the USSR. Soldiers and civilians alike waved, shouted, and cheered.

After all those dreary weeks, here at last was one sight they would want to remember.

A celebration in the streets of Stalingrad after the German surrender

Second Front

The *Wehrmacht* was to fight on stubbornly until May 8, 1945—V-E Day—the day of final Allied victory in Europe. But never again was success so nearly within Hitler's grasp as it had been that summer and early autumn of 1942.

Having lost their last chance with Rommel's defeat at El Alamein, the Nazis in North Africa surrendered to the Allied powers on May 12, 1943. This meant that from then on Hitler would have to fight defensively, confined to Europe.

The surrender in North Africa finished any hope Hitler might have had of someday reaching the oil fields of the Middle East. The retreat of Army Group A in the Russian Caucasus had deprived him of the oil fields at Baku. From now on the fuel he needed to power his mobile units on the ground and his fighters and bombers in the air would be in ever-diminishing supply.

One more critical battle remained to be fought on Russian soil, a gigantic clash of tanks that began on July 5, 1943, at Kursk. But the Russians were no longer outclassed. While Stalingrad held, tanks, planes, and guns were pouring out of the factories. At Kursk the Russians could face the invader on better than even terms. The battle ended in another conclusive Russian victory.

An Allied second front, so long dreaded by Hitler, became a reality at last. On D Day, June 6, 1944, Allied forces, under the command of General Dwight D. Eisenhower, crossed the English Channel and swarmed ashore on the beaches of Normandy, in the north of France.

Only once thereafter—during the Battle of the Bulge as the Allies advanced in Belgium—did the Germans even threaten to throw the Allied sweep off balance.

Hitler's dream of "a world dominated by Germans for a thousand years" had been blasted for all time.

Der Fuehrer himself did not live to see the last collapse. His own *Götterdämmerung* (Twilight of the Gods) took place on April 30, 1945. Although the circumstances are still shrouded in mystery, he is believed to have committed suicide in his Berlin bunker.

A few days afterward, General Chuikov, defender of Stalingrad, had the satisfaction of riding at the head of his columns into Berlin.

The long nightmare of Nazi Germany was over. The curtain had fallen on the greatest, most senseless and tragic folly of modern times.

The bastion of Stalingrad had proved to be the bastion of the world.

A mute spokesman for the many who fought after Stalingrad

Chronology

1939

AUG. 23.   The Russians and Germans sign a nonaggression pact.
SEPT. 3.   France and Great Britain declare war on Germany.

1940

MAY 10.   The Germans invade Belgium, Holland, and Luxemburg. Neville Chamberlain resigns, and Winston Churchill becomes Prime Minister of England.
DEC. 9.   The British 8th Army begins its offensive in North Africa.
DEC. 18.   Hitler decides to invade Russia.

1941

MAR. 31.   The Germans begin a counteroffensive in North Africa.
APR. 5.   The Russians and Yugoslavs sign a nonaggression pact.
MAY 6.   Josef Stalin becomes the head of the Russian government.
JUNE 22.   Germany invades Russia.
SEPT. 30.   The Germans begin their offensive against Moscow.
OCT. 25.   The first German offensive against Moscow fails.
OCT. 30.   The nine-month siege of Sebastopol begins.

NOV. 16.   A second offensive by the Germans against Moscow is launched.

DEC. 7.   The Japanese bomb Pearl Harbor, a United States naval base.

DEC. 8.   The United States and Great Britain declare war on Japan. The Japanese begin air raids on Midway, Guam, Hong Kong, and the Philippine Islands.

DEC. 11.   Hitler declares war on the United States.

1942

APR. 9.   The Allied troops on Bataan surrender.

MAY 6.   Corregidor, a United States island bastion in the Philippines, surrenders to the Japanese.

JUNE 19.   A German plane is shot down, and the Russians obtain Hitler's master plan for the attack against the Soviet Union.

JUNE 28.   The beginning of the German attack in the south of Russia. The British 8th Army retreats to El Alamein in Egypt.

JULY 13.   The German 4th Panzer Army is nearing Stalingrad when Hitler diverts it south—losing a good opportunity to capture the unprepared city.

JULY 28.   German units of Army Group A capture Rostov.

JULY 30.   Stalin issues his order to the Russian Army: "Not another step back."

AUG. 7.   The American forces land at Guadalcanal.

AUG. 12.   Winston Churchill and Averell Harriman arrive in Moscow to tell Stalin that there will be no second front immediately.

AUG. 23.   The first all-out attack on Stalingrad is launched. The Germans bomb the city, and 40,000 Russians are killed in the air raids.

SEPT. 10.   The Germans reach the Volga, splitting the 62nd and 64th Russian Armies.

SEPT. 13.   Another heavy German offensive begins, including air raids and tank attacks on Stalingrad.

SEPT. 24.   Most of the central section of Stalingrad has fallen into German hands.

OCT. 14.   The Germans begin their heaviest ground attack in the northern part of Stalingrad; it proves unsuccessful through the last days of October.

OCT. 23.   British and German forces meet in battle at El Alamein.

NOV. 4.   General Rommel's troops are defeated at El Alamein and begin their retreat.

NOV. 8.   The Allies begin to land in French North Africa.

NOV. 11.   The last German offensive in Stalingrad is launched by General Paulus.

NOV. 13.   The sea battle of Guadalcanal begins.

NOV. 19.   The Russians, led by General Vatutin, begin their counterattack by firing on the Rumanian troops about seventy-five miles from Stalingrad.

NOV. 22.   General Vatutin, coming from the north, and General Eremenko, coming from the south, meet at Kalach and surround 330,000 German soldiers located in and around Stalingrad.

NOV. 24.   The German generals trapped in Stalingrad ask permission to fight their way out. Hitler refuses because Hermann Goering, head of the Luftwaffe, promises to supply the troops by airlift.

DEC. 12.   General von Manstein begins a drive from the south in an attempt to break through to General Paulus.

DEC. 15.   Von Manstein crosses the Axai River.

DEC. 16.   General Vatutin routs the Italians on the Don River.

DEC. 23.   Von Manstein crosses the Myshkova.

DEC. 24.   General Malinovsky stops von Manstein within thirty miles of Stalingrad, and von Manstein begins a retreat which continues during the next month.

1943

JAN. 2.   Hitler orders Army Group A to withdraw from the Caucasus; they had been halted within sixty miles of the Baku oil fields. The Russians capture Pitomnik Airfield, drastically cutting the German airlift.

JAN. 8.   The Russians send General Paulus an ultimatum to surrender, which Hitler will not allow him to accept.

JAN. 17.   The surrender demand is repeated, but Paulus ignores it.

JAN. 23.   The Allied 8th Army arrives at Tripoli.

JAN. 31.   General Paulus surrenders.

FEB. 2.   The last isolated pockets of Germans in the north of the city surrender.

FOR FURTHER READING

Nonfiction

CHUIKOV, VASILI I. *The Battle for Stalingrad*. New York: Holt, Rinehart and Winston, 1964.

CLARK, ALAN. *Barbarossa*. London: Hutchinson, 1965.

GROSSMAN, VASSILI. *Stalingrad Hits Back*. Moscow: Foreign Languages Publishing House, 1942.

KERR, WALTER. *The Russian Army*. New York: Knopf, 1944.

ROONEY, ANDREW. *The Fortunes of War*. Boston: Little, Brown, 1962.

SCHROTER, HEINZ. *Stalingrad*. New York: Dutton, 1958.

SETH, RONALD. *Stalingrad: Point of Return*. London: Gollanz, 1959.

SHIRER, WILLIAM L. *The Rise and Fall of the Third Reich*. New York: Simon and Schuster, 1960.

WERTH, ALEXANDER. *Russia at War*, 1941-1945. New York: Dutton, 1964.

———. *The Year of Stalingrad*. London: H. Hamilton, 1946.

Fiction

GERLACH, HEINRICH. *The Forsaken Army*. New York: Harper, 1958.

PLIVIER, THEODOR. *Stalingrad*. London: Athenaeum, 1948.

SIMONOV, KONSTANTIN M. *Days and Nights*. New York: Simon and Schuster, 1945.

INDEX

Axai River, 24, 70, 71
Axis, 10, 11, 13, 15

Baku, 14, 17, 70, 89
Batyuk, General N. F., 45, 55
Bock, Marshal Fedor von, 17

Chuikov, General Vasili I., commands 64th Red Army, 23, 24; describes plight of Stalingrad, 27; made general of 62nd Army, 30–31; commands 64th Army's defense of Stalingrad, 30–35, 39–40, 45–46, 48–49, 52, 55; his *The Battle for Stalingrad* quoted, 31–32; describes fighting in city, 33; instructions for street fighting, 39–40; message to Khrushchev, 45; in "Bloody October" fighting, 48–49; tribute to women fighters, 52; enters Berlin, 90

Dimitrescu, Colonel General, 59
Don River, 20, 23

Ehrenburg, Ilya, 36
Eisenhower, General Dwight, 89
El Alamein, Battle of, 56, 89
Eremenko, General Andrei I., 60, 61

German Army (armies): Afrika Korps, 12–13, 56; launches *Blitzkrieg* in Russia, 13, 14; Army Group B, 16, 17, 19; Army Group A, 16–17, 19, 20, 21, 70, 82, 89; 4th Panzer (Tank), 17, 20, 25, 29, 70; 6th Army, 17, 25, 53–55, 68, 69, 74–87, 80–84, 86; moves toward Stalingrad, 19–24; in Stalingrad, 31–57; besieged in Stalingrad, 64–89; Army of the Don, 69–70, 71; Operation Winter Gale, 70; surrender of, 86–87
Goering, Hermann, 68, 69, 70
Gorishnyi, 50
Great Britain, 12, 13, 47
Gurtiev, Colonel L. N., 50

Hitler, Adolf, as German leader and strategist, 8–10, 12; fear of Great Britain and U.S.A., 13; and Stalin sign nonaggression pact, 13; Russian strategy of, 14–17, 19, 20; underestimates Russians, 23; orders air and Panzer attacks on Stalingrad, 25, 29; tank losses, 49; Paulus's message to, 53; learns of U.S. forces in North Africa, 56; determination to take Stalingrad, 57; attitude toward satellite troops, 59; reinforces Stalingrad front, 61; disregard for welfare of troops, 64; strategy for Stalingrad front, 68–70; and Mussolini, 72; orders Tormasin Group of Army of the Don northeast, 73; and Paulus, 79, 80, 83, 87; orders Army Group A to withdraw, 82; names Paulus Field Marshal, 86; communiqué admitting surrender of Stalingrad, 87; defeat in Russian and Western Europe, 89–90; death of, 90
Hoth, General Hermann, 17, 20, 29

Italian Army, 57, 72

Khrushchev, Nikita, 30, 45
Klimienko, Nadya, 52
Konning, Major, sniper, 43, 44
Konyukov, Sergeant Pyotr, 7, 8
Krieger, Eugene, 19–20, 30, 38–39, 60

Leonov, Lieutenant, 38–39
List, Marshal Siegmund, 17
Luftwaffe, airlift, 68–69, 76

Malinovsky, General Rodion, 71, 73–75
Manstein, General Erich von, 69–70, 71, 72, 73–75
Medvedev, Viktor, sniper, 42, 43

Myshkova River, 24, 70, 73

North Africa, 12–13, 47, 56, 89

Paulus, Field Marshal Friedrich von, commands German 6th Army, 17, 57, 59; launches last great offensive, 53–55; presents plan to Hitler, 68; refuses Manstein's order to meet him, 73; headquarters in Stalingrad, 79; gets Red Army ultimatum, 80, 83; surrenders, 85–86; and Rokossovsky, 87

Raske, Major General, 84–85
Red Army (armies): High Command gets plans for German offensive, 8–9; in 1919, 18; Stalin ordered to, 21; retreats in July, 1942, 21, 23; Cossacks, 22, 60–61; 62nd Army, 23, 29, 30, 84; 64th Army, 23, 29, 30; Russian War Council order to, 30; 2nd Guards Army, 34–36, 71, 74–75; Katyushas, at Stalingrad, 40–41, 55; women at war, 52; 118th Guards Regiment, 55; begins counterattack, 57; counteroffensive against Rumanian 3rd Army, 58–61; withdraws on Axai River front, 70; Air Force, 72; offensive in Stalingrad, 74–87 passim; airlift, 79; occupies Pitomnik Airfield, 82; on surrender of Stalingrad, 86; enters Berlin, 90
Rodimtsev, General Alexander Ilyich, 34–36, 45, 51
Rokossovsky, General Konstantin, 64, 80, 81–82, 86, 87
Rommel, General Erwin, 12–13, 47, 56, 89
Rumanian 3rd Army, 57, 58–61, 66, 67, 72, 73
Russian War Council, 20, 30, 45, 58–60, 75

Smekhotvorov, General F. N., 45
Stalin, Josef, 13, 18, 21, 25, 59
Stalingrad, Battle of, begins, 14, 15–16; description and history of, 16–19; Germans move toward, 19–24; becomes fortress, 24–25; partial evacuation of, 24, 25, 27; air raids on, 25; German armies close on, 25; Russians dig in at, 25–33; Chuikov in, 27, 30–35, 39–40, 45–46 48–49, 52, 55; Mamayev Hill in, 30–32, 34, 35, 36, 45, 55; Tsaritsa Ravine post in, 32, 46; Central Station fighting, 33, 36; "Rat War" in, 39–46; artillery at, 40–41; snipers in, 42–44; battle for factories in, 44–46, 50, 52, 53, 76; bombings of, 45; "Bloody October" fighting in, 47–53; losses from October offensive in, 49–50; Siberians in, 50; Red armies converge on, 61, 64; airfields under attack, 70; aftermath of, 86–88

United States of America, 13, 47, 56

Vasilievski, A. M., 59
Vatutin, General Nikolai, 58, 67, 72, 80, 81–82
Volga River, 23, 24, 25, 27, 29, 30, 32, 34, 38, 53, 55, 71, 79
Voronov, General Nikolai, 81
Vysokoostrovsky, war correspondent, 76

Weicks, General F. von, 17
Werth, Alexander, 85

Yelchenko, Lieutenant F., 84–86

Zaitsev, Vasili, 42, 43–44
Zeitzler, General Kurt, 68
Zholudev, 50
Zhukov, Georgi K., 59